boyhood, baggage and loving you

Koschei Bell

BookLeaf
Publishing
India | USA | UK

Presentation by *BookLeaf Publishing*

Web: www.bookleafpub.com

E-mail: info@bookleafpub.com

ISBN: 9789357446037

First edition 2022

boyhood freedom

A boyhood freedom I never had,
snatched away from my eager fingers.
Dirt under nails and cracked marker polish
and rough chewed edges.

So now I dye my hair.
Control that cannot be taken from me,
a freedom that cannot be taken from me,
reliving for the boy I never got to be.

This box is too big,
this box is too small,
no box is just right.
So I broke the walls of every one.

The boy I never got to be smiles now
when he looks at how far we've come,
how things have changed for us
and now he is free to exist a decade later.

My hair has been green like grass
and red like fire,
and blue like the colour of my favourite shirt
from when I was nine years old.

It had been black and brown,
and bright yellow and blonde.
some suit me some don't,
but that's not the point.

The little boy who was denied his existence,
he smiles at all the colours,
of the simple pleasure and impulsiveness of it,
of dying one's hair at 3am.

His eager fingers look a lot like mine,
just bigger now with less dirt.
But still chewed to quick and still painted,
still cracked black polish and gloss.

And we lay together,
watching the clouds,
getting grass stains on our jeans
and we talk.

He says he's proud of us,
of how far we've come together,
of all that's changed,
that he can finally be a part of me.

alchemy

Chemistry was never my strong suit.
I was much more of a star gazer than a potion
mixer
and I never liked the strong smell anyway.

She enjoyed the alchemy though, the wizardry.
She hated when I called her Merlin.
I was King Arthur and I would protect her,

from all those who would do her harm,
who would take her love of flames burning blue
and metal glowing bright and turn it against her.

Her passion will not be a weapon,
something in a game far bigger than the both of
us
far bigger than us as people.
As lovers.

The chemistry between us was far different from
that in a lab.
We had no guidelines of combustibles or
compounds
no way of predicting reactions between us

but we learned together.
I learned that she hated being called Merlin
and she'd hit me every time.

Chemistry was her thing, her passion, her love,
and I was the star gazer, the dreamer who
couldn't focus on what was in front of them.
I was stupid.
I miss the strong smell of chemicals in my head
and in my blood.

starkiller

He stood atop the world he'd build with bloody
hands,
and he smiled, knowing he did it all alone.
He didn't need their help, their broken tools,
their ideals,
he'd do it properly this time around.

His father was a failure and he wouldn't repeat
those mistakes.
He wouldn't be like that rotten man before him.
Everyone that told him he was crazy was now
proved wrong,
so why wouldn't the doubt leave him alone?

Deep down, he was scared he was exactly all he
hated,
that he had no heart or voice or human soul.
But that shouldn't matter when you sit upon a
throne,
built with anger and fire and brimstone.

His chest ached, empty,
void of something that was never there to begin
with,
and he walked in heavy paces,

his mind off somewhere he could never truly
see.

But he dreamed each night,
of a world in which he was understood,
where people looked at him
and saw more than darkness and dread.

But he was darkness, and he was dread.
All those haunting tales of him were true,
and the blood rolled down his knuckles, dripping
on his boots,
staining his shirt cuffs with honour and victory.

He was the starkiller.
Ruthless and destructive with no reservations.
He refused to be anything but that, he wouldn't.
For he'd tasted the power and would do
anything to keep it.

# of my own soul

This craving, this yearning,
This never ending burning.
All heated and fire,
All you are is a liar.

I trusted in you
But bit off more than I could chew.
My heart in your hands,
But I'm left in the badlands

Picking up the pieces you left behind.
Counting all those times that I cried,
Were some of the worst nights of my life,
Stabbing like a switchblade knife.

At night alone, I walked dark streets,
Anything not to climb into the sheets
Of our shared bed where you'd rest your head,
And slept like bricks of lead.

Because I was scared and I hate that you did
that,
Turned me into a fucking doormat
That you wiped your boots on after work,
All the while wearing that smirk

That you knew drove me crazy.
But I looked at you so hazy
With this love inside me
And I gave it to you all for free

Because you told me you deserved it.
But ever so slowly, I unlearned it,
I realised it just wasn't true,
That I did not belong to you.

I was a person of my own,
Body, mind and soul.
And once I was free,
You could not stop me.

And you were scared.
And so you should be.

rising above it

When he managed to surface, he gulped in air
he breathed in all he could because he didn't
know when he'd have the chance again.

His chest would ache, swell with the atmosphere
around him.
His throat would burn and set alight, and he let it
because what choice did he have.

Control was something he lost long ago,
something he wished to desperately regain but
with every try, he failed.
He fell even further, and it was harder to get up
each time.

He should be okay, he kept telling himself that,
over and over, but it never made a difference,
because every single time he tried to tell himself
he was fine he felt worse.

Parts inside of him cracked and crumbled, but
never died.
He wished those parts would die, then he'd
never feel this way again,

but his heart continued to beat, and it reminded
him each time that he was alive,
and he hated it.

He could go about his day and smile when
needed and listen when needed
and be there for them when they needed.
What he needed was peace that he knew he
would never get,
or noise he could never hear.

Everything was either excruciatingly loud or
deafeningly silent.
His head couldn't deal with it, jumps from the
extremes,
but that was his life now.
That was what it had become.

He fought against it so hard, he tried to be
alright,
he tried to smile and mean it and laugh and
mean it but he couldn't.
He wanted things to be the way they used to be
when he was happy.

Happy, a distant memory so far lost if didn't feel
real,
like a fever dream of hope and sunshine and
spring air.

It was winter for him, but one abandoned to the
cold.

The simple things became a task he didn't want
to complete or he couldn't complete.
He wanted it to be over.

Every day he woke up was a constant reminder
that he rose above it.
He wasn't always sure why he did, but maybe
fate knew something he didn't,
giving him a push in the right direction, the push
to keep on living,
to keep breathing and it hurt so much but he
breathed in anyway,
lungfuls of air.

And he flailed his limbs to keep afloat, it tired
him, but he did not stop.

sour

Breathing has become quite difficult for me.
Something about the air these days tastes sour to
me.
No one else can smell it,
and they look at me crazy when I mention it.

I can never seem to shake it, it lingers.
I think it's me sometimes, like I radiate it,
like it sticks to me like glue.
Makes me feel sick.

Shower after shower and bath after bath,
I try to rid the smell from me.
I think it's gone, but it comes back.
Still no one else can smell it.

It makes breathing hard, it makes speaking hard.
It even makes getting out of bed in the morning
hard.
No one seems to get it of course,
when I say I'm paralysed and choking.

The air tastes sour and so it stops me eating,
and it stops me drinking, stops me sleeping.

They don't get it, I know that, yet I keep trying
to explain.
I should give up, they'll never get it.

and I love you

I love it when you smile,
something always so rare but getting rarer still,
it fills me with a warmth no fire can give me.
And I love it when you laugh,
a sign you're truly comfortable,
and I only ever hear you laugh with me and me
alone.

But I hate it when you're busy,
because when you're busy, nothing else matters;
I'm nothing to you when your mind is on a task.
And it hate it when you leave,
days at a time and I'm lost without you,
not a single word to say you're safe.

But I love it when you surprise me,
coming home early and your arms are ready
to hold me for as long as we bear.
And I love it when it's quiet between us,
no words needed to express what we know
is real and solid.

But I hate it when you push me away,
too embarrassed or hurt or scared,
though I've never been less than there for you.

And I hate it when you doubt me,
like I don't already look at you like you're my
entire world,
which you are, and so much more.

But I love it when you tell me I'm special,
that I'm the only one who's seen this side of
you,
because I know you're the only one who's seen
this me too.
And I love it when you touch me,
I feel alive under your fingers as you kiss me,
the world goes silent around me.

we're not perfect

We're not perfect, we're not ever close,
but isn't that part of the fun?
That I look at you and see how flawed you are
but I love you anyway.

Your father was a bastard, deprived you of the
fundamental things.
Mine never stuck around long enough to care.
Your mother died when you were young,
and mine, she worked so hard that I never really
saw her.

It messed us up, these things, our broken
childhoods,
but it makes us, us, whether we like it or not.
And I wonder how different either of us would
be if things had been just a little more normal
but I don't dwell on that often.

Neither of us are close to perfect, but we try so
very hard to at least be good.
We try to be good people and really, we can't
ask for more.
I see you tried to be perfect, so perfect you're
inhuman,

but I love the things you call imperfections.

You cry at sad films and tap your feet to music,
and you absolutely adore romance more than
you think you should.
You sing in the shower and know flower types
more clearly than most,
and you will spend an hour matching your tie to
your socks.

All fuss you are sometimes, and I was too
impatient when I met you to appreciate all these
things.
I do now.
Like how you hate mushy peas and call me a pea
traitor for loving them
and how you refuse to let me leave the house
without combing my hair.

Neither of us perfect, but both of us perfect for
each other.
That's what matters in the end, or at least I think
so.
It's not how the world sees you,
it's how your world sees you.

And I love you more than anything.

lonely little boy

A small little boy, sat alone in the grass,
different from the others but content in that.
As content as a lonely boy could be.

He picks at the blades and picks them the pieces.
His trousers are dirty and shirt made of creases.
Quiet as he weaves a little bracelet.

Other children are playing and laughing with joy
while he sits alone with an old broken toy,
wanting to play but he can't.

Too nervous to speak, too nervous to stand,
to walk his way over and wave his small hand,
and so he watches with a sad little smile.

Maybe one day, the thinks, as he watches them run,
he'll pluck up the courage and go have some fun.
For now though, content as a lonely boy he is.

tied to things I can't control

Family dinner and I sit there,
listening to the same, dreaded questions.
"When are you getting a job?"
"When are you leaving?"
"When are you going to do something with your
life?"

I wish I knew.
I look but of course, nothing fits.
I try but nobody wants me.
How would that not drain you?

It keeps me awake sometimes, the anxiety,
the fear of what I won't become.
But every failure makes me scared, keeps me
halted,
until I can't take another step.

"It's not that hard," they said, but what would
they know,
born in a world long dead before I arrived.
And a world still dying now, dying by their
hands;

it's all connected, these feelings, my being

all tied to things I can't control.
My brain can't control itself, let alone anything
else.

A job would be nice, getting away, being myself.
But I'm stuck.
I'm trapped.
The more asking, demanding, the more probing
questions only makes the problem worse.

sweet little love

We step around each other, doing our odd little
dance.
It's rather fun, I will say that,
but sometimes I just wish to kiss you.

To sweep you up and hold you,
to love you until you tell me to stop,
and then I'll love you a little bit more

from afar because I'd never want to hurt you.
Of course, I'd never want to hurt you.
You are everything to me and I'd never want to
hurt you.

drenched

It rains, and I lay out in the road,
drenched.
I am cold and I hate the rain,
but I stay
unable to move
to breathe.
I stay alone, drenched in the rain.

Until you.

You don't try to pull me out from the road.
You don't give me an umbrella.
You don't shield me because you know I can't.

You lay with me.

It rains, and we lay out in the road,
drenched,
but not alone.
I am cold and a hate the rain,
but the warmth of you hand finds me,
grounds me,
helps me to breathe.

wonderland

Wandering through wonderland,
through a world of trees like giants,
through a world of purple ocean water,
through a world with magic and dreams.

An escape, they say, and maybe they're right,
for who'd want to live like here with a choice?
But this world isn't perfect and it's constantly
changing,
but it's a home like no other.

People still suffer and are sad and in pain
but there's always a silver lining to the storm
clouds.
There is always hope, it never dies,
as we all go play in the sun.

Mermaid and fairies and dragons in lairs,
knights in armour and goblins and witches.
Fantasy lands to run away to,
to pretend to be everything different.

We can be what we want to be,
we can live how we want to be,
and we can love how we want to be.

Simple things, not without pain, but the joy is
the most that we care for.

was rather a cherished thing

She said to her lover as the were wrapped up in
bed,
"my dear, you know I love you, don't you?"
To which he lover replied,
"I know you do, utterly and completely, for you
asked me the same thing yesterday."

"Oh," said the first, as her hold tightened softly,
legs entangled through the bedsheets,
the sun streaming in outside as the ay continued
on,
but neither had anywhere to be without the other.

"Oh indeed," the second then said, basking in the
warmth and the love,
the care and affection.
"I never tired of you asked though, since it's a
reminded all itself,
that you worry I might just forget."

She kissed tender skin, as she processed the
words, to what that could mean.

Her forgetfulness a reminder?
Seemed rather strange to her;
they'd been together so long, so utterly in love,
and yet little mysteries still existed.

Was rather a cherished thing.

"I don't worry you'll forget, just that maybe I
don't show it as well as I should."
"But I know you, or did you forget?
I know you better than anyone else, more than
yourself at times I fear,
but that's alright, since I love you."

"I fear it isn't hard to know me more than me."
Her finger drew shapes across her lover's belly,
like hearts and stars and little smiley faces.
It was close to noon, and they should get up, but
she held her in her arms,
and that was utterly enough.

"You don't give yourself enough credit, that's
what I think," as the first's hands were drawn up
to the second's lips,
gentle kisses against bruised knuckles.
An accident with a wall, too much all at once,
but happy all at once, just too much to process.

Kisses then to the ring on her finger,

simple and plain but what they'd disgusted what felt like years ago now.
Perfectly her and perfectly them.
"I love you," said the second, melting into safety.

"I love you too."

three piece suits

Weak for you in your three piece suits,
and you know it too that's why you dress in blue;
my favourite colour.

Weak for you and your charming smile,
beautifully crooked and wicked and wild;
drives me crazy.

Weak for you and the way that you talk,
all proper and accented and perfect to a fault;
read to me.

Weak for you with your dumb little ties,
colours, patterns, all bright and ugly on the eyes;
but soft on you.

Weak for you and the way that you laugh,
when you really let go and you just can't hold it
back;
it's contagious.

Weak for you and all that you do,
dream through the day and I stare up at the
moon and think;
him.

it's always you

It's so loud,
too loud,
I can't breath,
can't think,
but can't escape,
held in place by you.

You, you…
Why won't you let me go?
It hurts,
and you know it.
You know it hurts me,
but you make me stay.

Builds character,
builds strength you say.
Only teaches me you aren't a friend.
Not a friend,
an enemy,
a looming nightmare.

Over and over
I plead to you.
You don't listen or don't care.
Or both.

I stop trying,
no air to get the words out.

Is it fun for you?
Do you get a kick out of it?
Watching me suffer?
I don't know,
too scared to ask,
to know that you do.

Maybe one day,
but not today.
Today I hide and hope.
Hope to drown things out,
for silence,
for air.

dumb little love poems

Dumb little love poems, that's what they are,
and I'm not all that good at them either.
They're silly and clumsy and rather a mess,
but I promise I'm trying really hard.

I think that you'll like them, if I ever work up
the nerve
to show you in person, the love and the words.
Maybe you won't but I hope that you see
that I really am trying to make it work.

You can tell I'm not at all made for this,
with limited skills and writing technique,
but I really do mean the clumsy things that I say,
that I love you, I love you, I love you.

find you

I'll probably never get to tell you in person,
that without you, my life would be something far
different.

I have memories of you so clear that they feel
almost real,
and I have to remind myself that they aren't
memories,
only dreams.
I look at the sky and I feel you beside me,
but I know you aren't there,
just the wish that you could enjoy the colours
above as much as me.

And I find comfort in you, though you are miles
away,
time zones apart but that doesn't seem like it
matters,
your voice carrying words to me in an instant.
And this warmth surrounds me,
like ice would melt to puddles,
and I'm reminded how special you make me
feel.

I know things are different for you now,

the change taking time to settle,
but know that I still care.
I wish I could tell you this,
that you know I'm not lying or saying what you
think I should,
but I care more than you know.

not her

You see her when you look at me.
We look alike, I know that, I can't change my
face,
but I tell you things are different now,
but you won't listen.

It was blissful ignorance before, that you didn't
know you were getting it wrong.
You know now,
but you still do it,
and have the nerve to look at me like I am
wrong.

I'm not.

I know who I am, who I'm not, who you wish I
was.
I never was who you wish I was,
never perfect enough for you,
and yet you still see her when you look at me.

It hurts, that you don't see me.
You see through me if at all.
I feel less than human because of you
sometimes.

It is terrifying to lose myself to you.

I won't, I hold on too tight,
but you don't see how my knuckles go white,
fighting to just be me and not her.
Why can't you see?

You chose not to see.

Blue eyes and brown hair, and the same round
face.
The same height, wardrobe overlap,
the same accent when I talk.
I don't deny the similarities but you deny the
differences.

I am happier. I am freer.
I am the person I was born to be, not her.
Different way of holding myself, of living,
different struggles I can't tell you because you
clam up.

Can't dare be anything but her.

If you lose me to her,
it's your fault alone.